DISCOVERING
STEGOSAURUS

BY LAURA HAMILTON WAXMAN

AMICUS | AMICUS INK

Sequence is published by Amicus and Amicus Ink
P.O. Box 1329, Mankato, MN 56002
www.amicuspublishing.us

Copyright © 2019 Amicus. International copyright reserved in all countries. No part of this book may be reproduced in any form without written permission from the publisher.

Library of Congress Cataloging-in-Publication Data
Names: Waxman, Laura Hamilton, author.
Title: Discovering Stegosaurus / by Laura Hamilton Waxman.
Description: Mankato, Minnesota : Amicus, [2019] | Series: Sequence. Discovering Dinosaurs | Audience: K to grade 3. | Includes bibliographical references and index.
Identifiers: LCCN 2017034372 (print) | LCCN 2017040865 (ebook) | ISBN 9781681515182 (pdf) | ISBN 9781681514369 (library binding) | ISBN 9781681523569 (pbk.) | ISBN 9781681515182 (ebook)
Subjects: LCSH: Stegosaurus--Juvenile literature. | Dinosaurs--Juvenile literature.
Classification: LCC QE862.O65 (ebook) | LCC QE862.O65 W39 2019 (print) | DDC 567.915/3--dc23
LC record available at https://lccn.loc.gov/2017034372

Editor: Rebecca Glaser
Designer: Aubrey Harper
Photo Researcher: Holly Young

Photo Credits: Shutterstock/Linda Bucklin, cover, Herschel Hoffmeyer, 4-5, Catmando, 6-7, Michael Rosskothen, 28-29; iStock, 5; Flickr/Mark Byzewski, 8-9, James St. John, 26-27; Getty/Colin Keates/Dorling Kindersley, 10-11, Arthur Dorety, 14-15, De Agostini Picture Library, 18-19, Corey Ford, 24-25; Corbis, 12-13; WikiCommons/Denver Museum of Nature and Science, 16-17; F.E. Warren Air Force Base/Matt Bilden, 20-21; Alamy/Andy Morton, 22-23

Printed in China

HC 10 9 8 7 6 5 4 3 2 1
PB 10 9 8 7 6 5 4 3 2 1

TABLE OF CONTENTS

Meet the Stegosaurus	5
Discovery!	9
Finding Stegosaurus's Family	13
Digging Up More	17
Recent Finds	22
Using Technology	29

Glossary	30
Read More	31
Websites	31
Index	32

Stegosaurus was 13 feet (3.9 m) tall and had a spiked tail.

Meet the Stegosaurus

The Stegosaurus lived 155 million years ago. It is known for the pointed **plates** along its neck and back. This dinosaur was about the size of a bus. It stretched 30 feet (9 m) long. Its back was 9 feet (2.7 m) tall. But the biggest plate added 4 feet (1.2 m). That made it as tall as a giraffe!

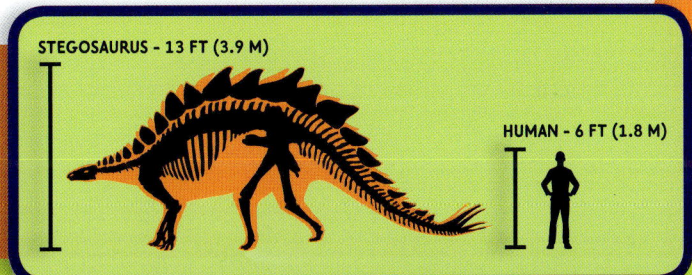

Stegosauruses roamed North America. They were in other parts of the world, too. They lived during the **Jurassic Period**. There were thick forests and many plants. These dinosaurs had small teeth. They liked tender, leafy greens. About 140 million years ago, Stegosauruses suddenly died out. They became **extinct**.

Two Stegosauruses search for plants to eat.

The Stegosaurus dies out.

140 MILLION YEARS AGO

..LOADING..LOADING..

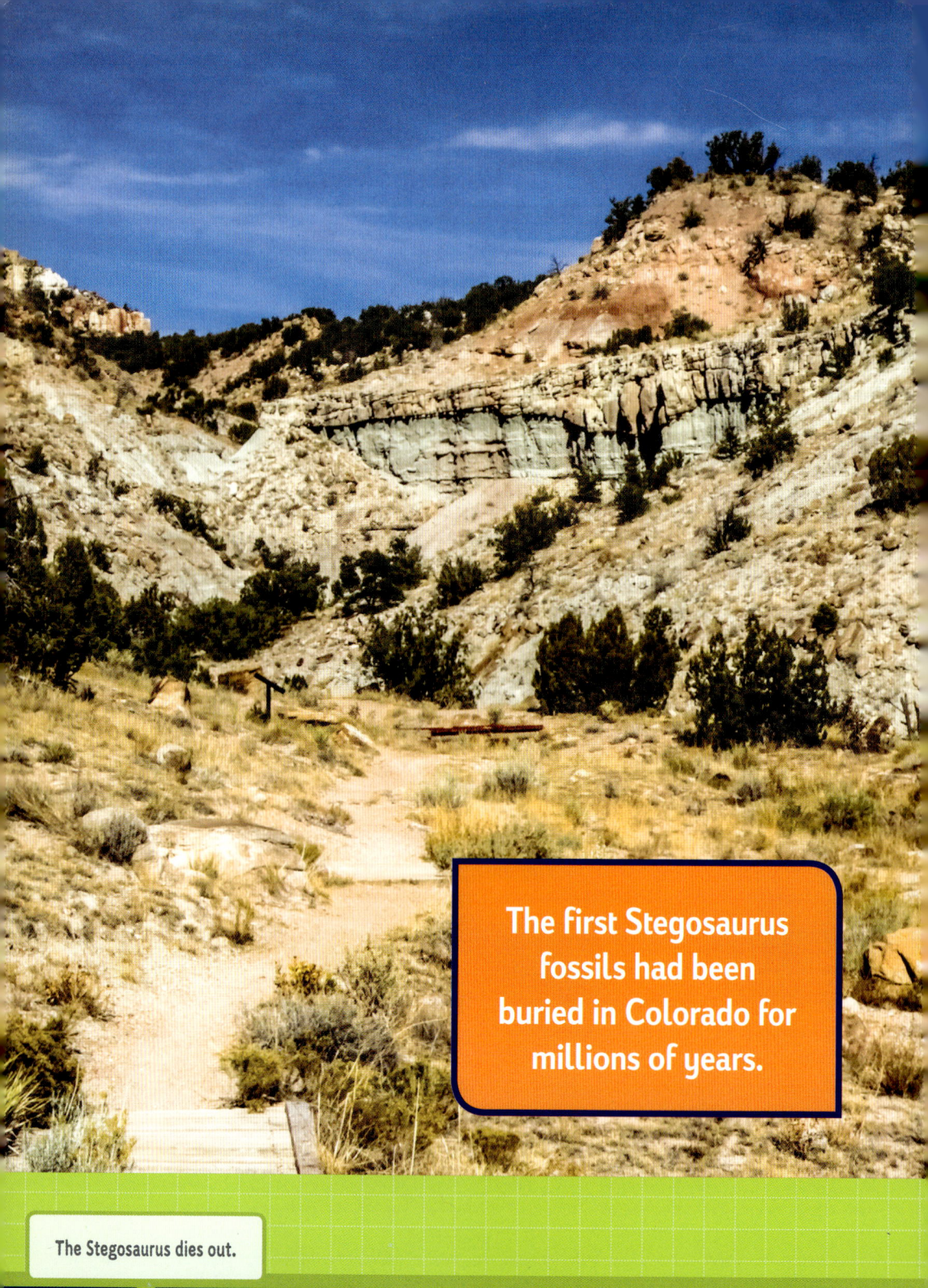

The first Stegosaurus fossils had been buried in Colorado for millions of years.

The Stegosaurus dies out.

140 MILLION YEARS AGO

1876

M.P. Felch discovers the first Stegosaurus fossils in Colorado.

Discovery!

In 1876, M.P. Felch was digging near his Colorado ranch. He found part of a strange **skeleton**. A **paleontologist** named O.C. Marsh studied the **fossils**. They were unlike any other bones he had ever seen. These were the first Stegosaurus fossils found!

Arthur Lakes discovered similar bones in Wyoming. He found part of a huge tail and some back plates. Marsh thought the plates formed a shell, as if it were a giant turtle. He believed they overlapped like shingles on a roof. In 1877, he named it Stegosaurus. This means "roof lizard."

This back plate has been worn down over time.

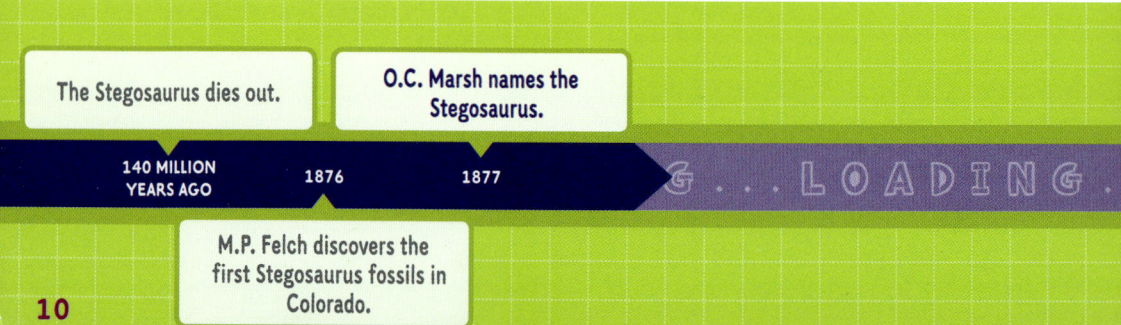

Bones like these helped scientists discover what Stegosaurus looked like.

The Stegosaurus dies out.		O.C. Marsh names the Stegosaurus.	
140 MILLION YEARS AGO	1876	1877	1879
	M.P. Felch discovers the first Stegosaurus fossils in Colorado.		Stegosaurus fossils prove it was a dinosaur.

Finding Stegosaurus's Family

In 1879, Lakes found part of another Stegosaurus. This skeleton had more bones. It was a dinosaur, not a turtle! Other **species** were soon found. They became part of the stegosaurid **family**. These dinosaurs walked on four legs. They all had bony back plates. They also had long spikes on their tails.

In 1886, fossil hunters dug out another skeleton in Colorado. This one was almost whole. The skull, plates, and tail were all in place. Its back plates stood up! Scientists now knew better what Stegosaurus looked like. It had a tiny head. Its brain was about the size of a plum!

Stegosaurus had two rows of back plates.

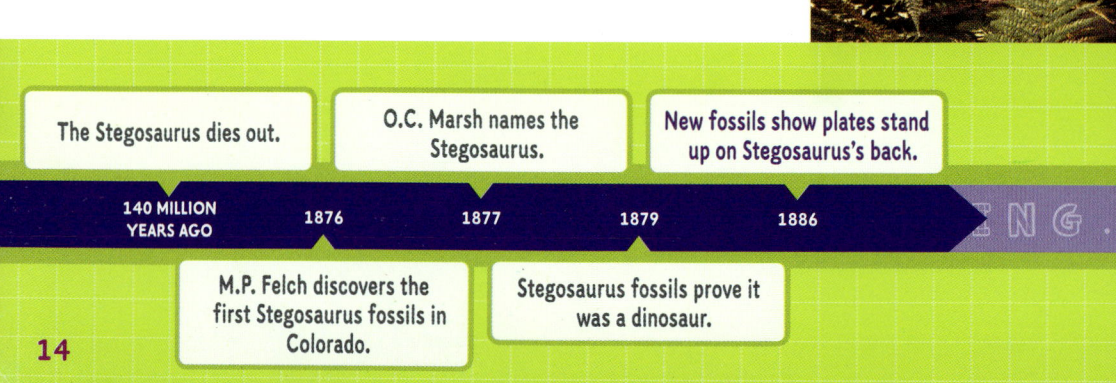

Skeletons like these are in museums for everyone to see.

The Stegosaurus dies out.	O.C. Marsh names the Stegosaurus.		New fossils show plates stand up on Stegosaurus's back.	
140 MILLION YEARS AGO	1876	1877	1879	1886	1937
	M.P. Felch discovers the first Stegosaurus fossils in Colorado.		Stegosaurus fossils prove it was a dinosaur.		Frank Kessler and his students discover the Colorado state fossil.

16

Digging Up More

In 1937, Frank Kessler took his class on a hike in Garden Park, Colorado. They found some dinosaur bones! It was the second Stegosaurus to be found there. This skeleton was later named the state fossil. It is on display in a Colorado **museum**.

In 1977, fossil hunters in Colorado found a young Stegosaurus. They dug out leg bones, shoulders, and hips. They found some ribs and pieces of the skull. No plates were there. Scientists think maybe plates formed as they grew up. It is the most complete **juvenile** skeleton!

As Stegosaurus got older, its plates grew bigger.

The Stegosaurus dies out.	O.C. Marsh names the Stegosaurus.	New fossils show plates stand up on Stegosaurus's back.
140 MILLION YEARS AGO	1876 — 1877 — 1879	1886 — 1937
	M.P. Felch discovers the first Stegosaurus fossils in Colorado.	Stegosaurus fossils prove it was a dinosaur.	Frank Kessler and his students discover the Colorado state fossil.

1977

Paleontologists find the most complete juvenile Stegosaurus.

The Stegosaurus dies out.	O.C. Marsh names the Stegosaurus.	New fossils show plates stand up on Stegosaurus's back.

140 MILLION YEARS AGO — 1876 — 1877 — 1879 — 1886 — 1937

M.P. Felch discovers the first Stegosaurus fossils in Colorado.	Stegosaurus fossils prove it was a dinosaur.	Frank Kessler and his students discover the Colorado state fossil.

In 1992, Bryan Small went fossil hunting in Colorado. He discovered the neck bone of another Stegosaurus. Its throat was covered with quarter-sized bones. They were like armor. They were preserved in place, just as in real life! This was the first discovery of its kind. The skeleton was one of the most complete yet.

The small bones covering Stegosaurus's throat might have been for protection.

New fossil shows Stegosaurus throat armor.

1977   1992

Paleontologists find the most complete juvenile Stegosaurus.

Recent Finds

In 2003, Bob Simon was digging a ditch on his Wyoming ranch. He discovered a Stegosaurus. Its bones were almost fully connected. This skeleton was almost complete. The skull was in excellent shape. It is one of the best dinosaur skulls ever found!

The Stegosaurus dies out.		O.C. Marsh names the Stegosaurus.		New fossils show plates stand up on Stegosaurus's back.	
140 MILLION YEARS AGO	1876	1877	1879	1886	1937
	M.P. Felch discovers the first Stegosaurus fossils in Colorado.		Stegosaurus fossils prove it was a dinosaur.		Frank Kessler and his students discover the Colorado state fossil.

Scientists can learn the most from complete skeletons.

New fossil shows Stegosaurus throat armor.

1977　　1992　　2003　　...LOADING...

Paleontologists find the most complete juvenile Stegosaurus.

The most complete Stegosaurus skeleton is found in Wyoming.

Stegosaurus lived in North America and Europe.

The Stegosaurus dies out.	O.C. Marsh names the Stegosaurus.		New fossils show plates stand up on Stegosaurus's back.	
140 MILLION YEARS AGO	1876	1877	1879	1886	1937
	M.P. Felch discovers the first Stegosaurus fossils in Colorado.		Stegosaurus fossils prove it was a dinosaur.		Frank Kessler and his students discover the Colorado state fossil.

24

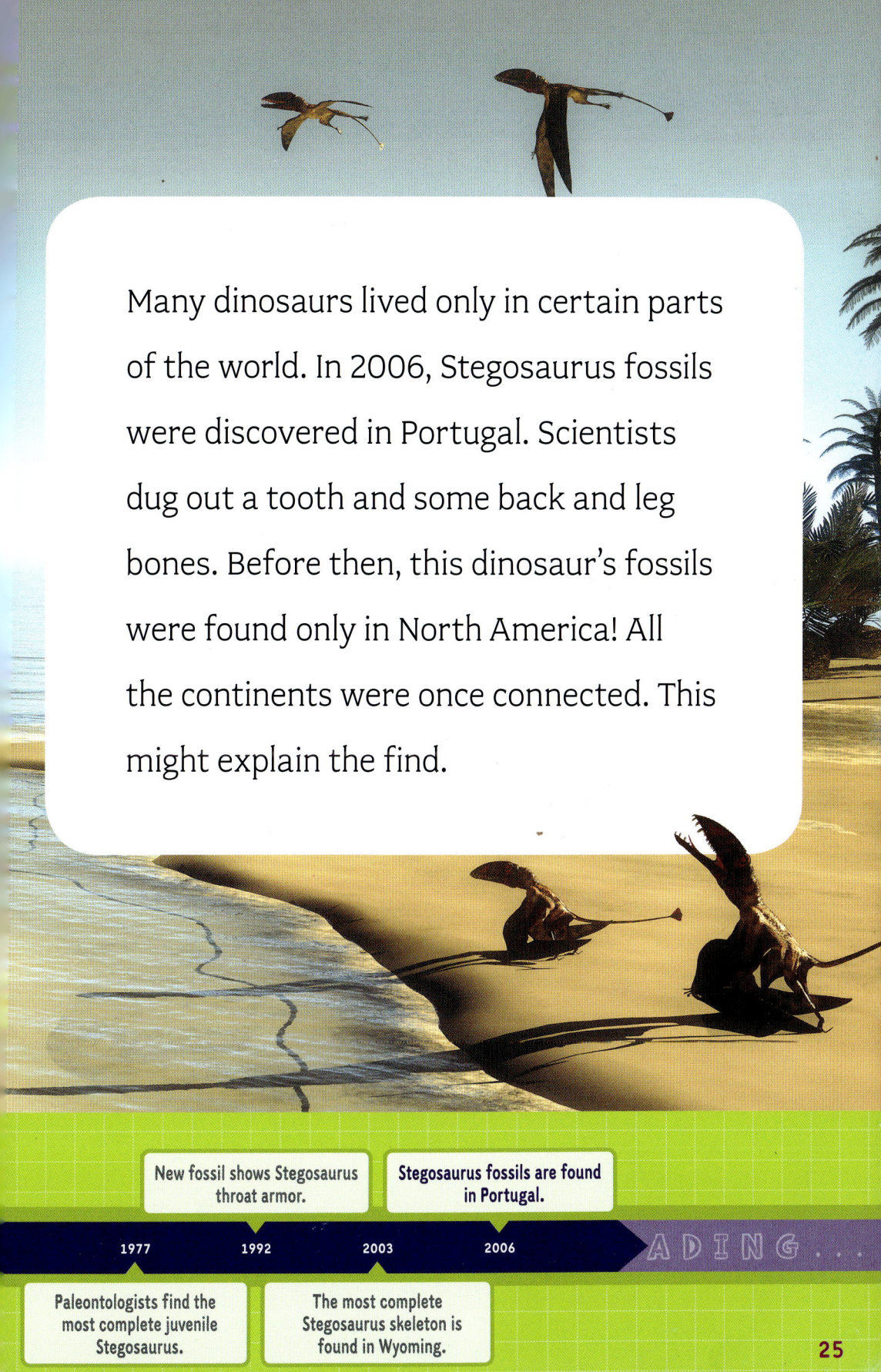

Many dinosaurs lived only in certain parts of the world. In 2006, Stegosaurus fossils were discovered in Portugal. Scientists dug out a tooth and some back and leg bones. Before then, this dinosaur's fossils were found only in North America! All the continents were once connected. This might explain the find.

New fossil shows Stegosaurus throat armor.

Stegosaurus fossils are found in Portugal.

1977   1992   2003   2006

Paleontologists find the most complete juvenile Stegosaurus.

The most complete Stegosaurus skeleton is found in Wyoming.

In 2007, paleontologist Matt Mossbrucker made a rare find. He discovered two tiny footprints in a rock. They were baby Stegosaurus tracks! They were about the size of a quarter. These were the first **hatchling** prints ever found! They showed a baby Stegosaurus was about the size of a cat.

> This close-up photo shows a track made by a baby Stegosaurus.

140 MILLION YEARS AGO	1876	1877	1879	1886	1937
The Stegosaurus dies out.		O.C. Marsh names the Stegosaurus.		New fossils show plates stand up on Stegosaurus's back.	
	M.P. Felch discovers the first Stegosaurus fossils in Colorado.		Stegosaurus fossils prove it was a dinosaur.		Frank Kessler and his students discover the Colorado state fossil.

26

| 1977 | 1992 | 2003 | 2006 | 2007 |

- 1992: New fossil shows Stegosaurus throat armor.
- 2006: Stegosaurus fossils are found in Portugal.
- 1977: Paleontologists find the most complete juvenile Stegosaurus.
- 2003: The most complete Stegosaurus skeleton is found in Wyoming.
- 2007: Hatchling footprints are discovered in Colorado.

27

Some scientists think that the Stegosaurus may have been able to stand on its back legs.

The Stegosaurus dies out.		O.C. Marsh names the Stegosaurus.			New fossils show plates stand up on Stegosaurus's back.	
140 MILLION YEARS AGO	1876	1877	1879	1886		1937
	M.P. Felch discovers the first Stegosaurus fossils in Colorado.		Stegosaurus fossils prove it was a dinosaur.			Frank Kessler and his students discover the Colorado state fossil.

Using Technology

Dinosaur footprints can be hard to study. A flat picture cannot show depth. Scientists now use **photogrammetry** to see 3D images. In 2014, Mossbrucker studied the hatchling tracks this way. Footprint fossils are different than bones. They can show how a dinosaur moved. What will scientists learn next?

GLOSSARY

extinct No longer living anywhere in the world.

family A group of related species with common features, used by scientists to classify animals.

fossil The remains of an animal or plant from millions of years ago that have turned into rock.

hatchling A newly hatched animal.

Jurassic Period A time during the Age of Dinosaurs from about 208 to 145 million years ago; the weather at this time was hot and humid.

juvenile Young.

museum A place where people go to see objects of art, science, or history.

paleontologists Scientists who study fossils.

photogrammetry A computer program that allows people to see photos in 3D.

plates Huge, pointy bones that grow on the neck, back, and tails of stegosaurids.

skeleton The complete set of bones from one animal.

species A group for animal or plant classification. Members of the same species can mate and have young.

READ MORE

Carr, Aaron. *Stegosaurus.* New York: Smartbook Media, Inc., 2018.

Holtz, Thomas, Jr. *Digging for Stegosaurus.* North Mankato, Minn.: Capstone Press, 2015.

Wegwerth, A.L. *Stegosaurus.* North Mankato, Minn.: Capstone Press, 2015.

WEBSITES

Easy Science for Kids | Stegosaurus Facts
http://easyscienceforkids.com/stegosaurus-facts-for-kids-video

Kids Dinos | Stegosaurus
www.kidsdinos.com/dinos/stegosaurus

Kids Dinosaurs | Stegosaurus Dinosaur
www.kids-dinosaurs.com/stegosaurus-dinosaur.html

National Geographic Kids | Stegosaurus
http://kids.nationalgeographic.com/animals/stegosaurus

Every effort has been made to ensure that these websites are appropriate for children. However, because of the nature of the Internet, it is impossible to guarantee that these sites will remain active indefinitely or that their contents will not be altered.

INDEX

3D, 29

Colorado, 8, 9, 14, 17, 18, 21

extinct, 6

Felch, M.P., 9
footprints, 26, 29

hatchlings, 26, 29

Jurassic Period, 6
juvenile, 18

Kessler, Frank, 17

Lakes, Arthur, 10, 13

Marsh, O.C., 9, 10

Mossbrucker, Matt, 26, 29
museum, 16, 17

North America, 6, 25

photogrammetry, 29
plates, 4, 5, 10, 13, 14, 18
Portugal, 25

Simon, Bob, 22
size, 5, 14, 21, 26
skeleton, 9, 13, 14, 16, 18, 22, 23
skull, 14, 18, 22
Small, Bryan, 21
species, 13
stegosaurid, 13

teeth, 6

ABOUT THE AUTHOR

Laura Hamilton Waxman has written and edited many nonfiction books for children. She loves learning about new things and sharing what she's learned with her readers. She lives in St. Paul, Minnesota.